TO:

FROM:

Illustrations copyright © 2011 Josephine Wall

Designed by Margaret Rubiano

Copyright © 2011
Peter Pauper Press, Inc.
202 Mamaroneck Avenue
White Plains, NY 10601
All rights reserved
ISBN 978-1-4413-0521-3
Printed in China
7 6 5 4 3

Visit us at www.peterpauper.com

The Spirit of Flight

BELIEVING IN OURSELVES

Introduction

"Fantasy gives me the opportunity to portray the world as I would like it to be," says artist Josephine Wall, who paints in a wisteria-covered cottage studio in Dorset, England, very near the sea. From early on, paintress Jo has had a passion for light, color, nature, and myth, and a wish "to inspire in her audience a personal journey into the magical world of their own imagination." Here, her enchanting artwork is combined with uplifting quotations, providing an illuminating feast for eye and soul. Let this little book of beauty and wisdom help you fly as far as your wings will take you!

Magic is believing in yourself. If you can do that, you can make anything happen.

JOHANN WOLFGANG VON GOETHE

The light of starry
dreams can only be
seen once we escape
the blinding cities
of disbelief.

SHAWN PURVIS

Faerie is never very far away . . . and there are a thousand ways of getting there.

SUSANNA CLARKE

*Millions of spiritual
creatures walk
the earth*

*Unseen, both when
we wake and when
we sleep.*

JOHN MILTON, *Paradise Lost*

"Well, now that we *have* seen each other," said the Unicorn, "if you believe in me, I'll believe in you. Is that a bargain?"

LEWIS CARROLL

It is the season
now to go

About the country
high and low,

Among the lilacs
hand in hand,

And two by two
in fairy land.

ROBERT LOUIS STEVENSON

To hope and dream is
not to ignore the practical.
It is to dress it in colors
and rainbows.

ANNE WILSON SCHAEF

I avoid looking forward
or backward, and try to
keep looking upward.

CHARLOTTE BRONTË

*To fly, we have
to have resistance.*

MAYA LIN

*Spread your wings
and let the fairy
in you fly!*

AUTHOR UNKNOWN

Vision is the art of seeing things invisible.

JONATHAN SWIFT

It's easy to believe in magic when you're young. Anything you couldn't explain was magic then. It didn't matter if it was science or a fairy tale. Electricity and elves were both infinitely mysterious and equally possible—elves probably more so.

CHARLES DE LINT

Our remedies oft in
ourselves do lie, Which
we ascribe to heaven.

WILLIAM SHAKESPEARE,
All's Well that Ends Well

Reach high, for stars lie hidden in your soul. Dream deep, for every dream precedes the goal.

PAMELA VAULL STARR

If we opened our minds to enjoyment, we might find tranquil pleasures spread about us on every side. We might live with the angels that visit us on every sunbeam, and sit with the fairies who wait on every flower.

SAMUEL SMILES

Earth's
crammed with
Heaven.

ELIZABETH BARRETT
BROWNING

Plant your own garden and decorate your own soul, instead of waiting for someone to bring you flowers.

VERONICA A. SHOFFSTALL

It's time to start living
the life you've imagined.

HENRY JAMES

Seeing is not believing; believing is seeing! You see things, not as they are, but as you are.

ERIC BUTTERWORTH

Whatever you can do,
or dream you can do,
begin it. Boldness has
genius, power, and
magic in it. Begin it!

AUTHOR UNKNOWN

Stories are like fairy gold.
The more you give away,
the more you have.

POLLY McGuire

Do not ask questions
of fairy tales.

JEWISH PROVERB

Remember that it takes many stars to light the night sky.

AUTHOR UNKNOWN

Sometimes I've believed as many as six impossible things before breakfast.

LEWIS CARROLL

If every day is an
awakening, you will
never grow old. You will
just keep growing.

GAIL SHEEHY

*We must overcome
the notion that we must
be regular . . . it robs
you of the chance to
be extraordinary.*

UTA HAGEN

Let yourself be silently
drawn by the strange pull
of what you really love.
It will not lead you astray.

R U M I

First you jump off
the cliff and you build
your wings on the
way down.

RAY BRADBURY

Angels fly because they take themselves lightly.

G. K. CHESTERTON

One's destination
is never a place, but
rather a new way of
looking at things.

HENRY MILLER

Not knowing when
the dawn will come,
I open every door.

EMILY DICKINSON

To every thing
there is a season, and a
time to every purpose
under the heaven.

ECCLESIASTES 3:1

When it is dark enough,
you can see the stars.

RALPH WALDO EMERSON

I arise today
Through the strength of heaven:
Light of sun,
Radiance of moon,
Splendour of fire,
Speed of lightning,
Swiftness of wind,
Depth of sea,
Stability of earth,
Firmness of rock.

"The Deer's Cry,"
ATTRIBUTED TO ST. PATRICK

Your love is a
strong force. It lightens
that which presumes to
weigh you down.

SOPHIA BEDFORD-PIERCE

*Nothing can
dim the light which
shines from within.*

MAYA ANGELOU

The most beautiful thing we can experience is the mysterious.

ALBERT EINSTEIN

A dream is a prophecy in miniature.

TALMUD

We are all part of
creation, all kings, all
poets, all musicians;
we have only to open up,
to discover what is
already there.

HENRY MILLER

*Where you believe
there is magic . . .
you will find it.*

AUTHOR UNKNOWN

Perhaps I am stronger
than I think.

THOMAS MERTON

We are such stuff as dreams are made on.

WILLIAM
SHAKESPEARE

*And above all, watch
with glittering eyes the
whole world around you
because the greatest secrets
are always hidden in the
most unlikely places.
Those who don't believe in
magic will never find it.*

ROALD DAHL

To play great music,
you must keep your
eyes on a distant star.

YEHUDI MENUHIN

I am not afraid of
storms for I am learning
how to sail my ship.

LOUISA MAY ALCOTT

If you can walk,
you can dance.
If you can talk,
you can sing.

ZIMBABWE PROVERB

Cherish your visions and your dreams as they are the children of your soul; the blueprints of your ultimate achievements.

NAPOLEON HILL

Our spirits soar on
the wings of angels.

SARAH MICHELLE

Follow your bliss and don't be afraid, and doors will open where you didn't know they were going to be.

JOSEPH CAMPBELL

You are a child of
the universe, no less
than the trees and the
stars; you have a
right to be here.

DESIDERATA

Dreams are
the touchstones of
our character.

HENRY DAVID THOREAU

Trust in dreams
for in them is hidden
the gate to eternity.

KAHLIL GIBRAN

*Happiness is reflective,
like the light of heaven.*

WASHINGTON IRVING

Let your life lightly dance
on the edges of Time like
dew on the tip of a leaf.

RABINDRANATH TAGORE

If you hear a voice within you say "you cannot paint," then by all means paint, and that voice will be silenced.

VINCENT VAN GOGH

To practice magic is
to bear the responsibility
for having a vision, for
we work magic by
envisioning what we
want to create.

STARHAWK

Be happy for this moment. This moment is your life.

OMAR KHAYYAM

Happiness is like a butterfly which, when pursued, is always beyond our grasp, but, if you will sit down quietly, may alight upon you.

NATHANIEL HAWTHORNE

*Some things
have to be believed
to be seen.*

RALPH HODGSON

*It is only with
the heart that one
can see rightly.*

ANTOINE DE SAINT-EXUPÉRY

Light tomorrow
with today.

**ELIZABETH BARRETT
BROWNING**

Life itself is the most wonderful fairy tale.

HANS CHRISTIAN ANDERSON

Illustrations

Visit the artist at
www.josephinewall.com